P9-CAO-897

America's **Westward** Expansion

California and the Southwest Join the United States

Christy Steele

WORLD ALMANAC® LIBRARY

Please visit our web site at: www.worldalmanaclibrary.com
For a free color catalog describing World Almanac® Library's list of high-quality books
and multimedia programs, call 1-800-848-2928 (USA) or 1-800-387-3178 (Canada).
World Almanac® Library's fax: (414) 332-3567.

Library of Congress Cataloging-in-Publication Data

Steele, Christy, 1970-
　　California and the Southwest join the United States / by Christy Steele.
　　　　p. cm. — (America's westward expansion)
　　Includes bibliographical references and index.
　　ISBN 0-8368-5786-0 (lib. bdg.)
　　ISBN 0-8368-5793-3 (softcover)
　　1. California—History—To 1846—Juvenile literature. 2. California—History—
1846-1850—Juvenile literature. 3. Southwest, New—History—Juvenile literature.
4. United States—Territorial expansion—Juvenile literature. I. Title.
　　F864.S697　2005
　　979.4'01—dc22　　　　　　　　　　　　　　　　　　　　　　　　2004056770

First published in 2005 by
World Almanac® Library
330 West Olive Street, Suite 100
Milwaukee, WI　53212　USA

Copyright © 2005 by World Almanac® Library.

Produced by: EMC—The Education Matters Company
Editors: Christy Steele, Rachael Taaffe
Designer and page production: Jennifer Pfeiffer
Maps and diagrams: Jennifer Pfeiffer
World Almanac® Library editorial direction: Mark J. Sachner
World Almanac® Library art direction: Tammy West
World Almanac® Library production: Jessica Morris
World Almanac® Library editors: Monica Rausch, Carol Ryback

Photo credits: Corbis: 22, 40; Library of Congress: cover, 4, 5, 6, 8, 9, 10, 11, 12, 14–15, 16,
18, 20, 23, 28, 29, 34, 36, 39, 44; National Archives: 24, 26, 31, 32, 33, 37, 38, 41, 42.

All rights reserved. No part of this book may be reproduced, stored in a retrieval system,
or transmitted in any form or by any means, electronic, mechanical, photocopying, recording,
or otherwise, without the prior written permission of the copyright holder.

Printed in Canada

1 2 3 4 5 6 7 8 9 09 08 07 06 05

Contents

Chapter 1

Spain and the Southwest

At the time of its birth, the United States consisted of thirteen states in eastern North America. Not content with its small size, the new nation quickly began acquiring more territory.

In 1823, U.S. President James Monroe firmly stated the nation's expansionist belief in the Monroe Doctrine. He staked U.S. claim to North America by telling European leaders, "Stay out of the Western Hemisphere."

The era of U.S. westward expansion was further fueled by the belief in Manifest Destiny. In 1845, writer John O'Sullivan first used this term to assert Americans' God-given right to take over the continent and spread U.S. ideas and government to new peoples and territories along the way.

Convinced of Manifest Destiny, thousands of people journeyed west-

◀ President James Monroe believed in expansion and helped negotiate the Louisiana Purchase. He felt that no European colonies should be allowed in North America.

ward. American settlers soon learned that people in the Southwest had a rich language, history, and culture of their own.

New Spain

Spain dominated southwestern culture during its several hundred years of Spanish rule. The Spanish-owned area of the Americas, including present-day Mexico, the U.S. Southwest (Texas, New Mexico, Arizona, Oklahoma, Nevada, and California) was called "New Spain."

Spanish leaders wanted to find a route to Asia by sea and hoped the key to this passage was somewhere in the northern frontier area of New Spain, today known as the U.S. Southwest. They explored the region to find the passage and to search for the Seven Cities of Cíbola, legendary cities containing amazing riches that were rumored to be in the interior of North America.

Colonization

In the early 1500s, Spain founded its empire in North

▲ A drawing of Andrew Jackson as a soldier in the War of 1812.

After John O'Sullivan first used the term Manifest Destiny, many other American leaders also began to write about it. Their goal was to convince Americans that the United States should expand across the continent to the Pacific Ocean. President Andrew Jackson asked Americans, "What good man would prefer a country covered with forest and ranged by a few thousand savages to our extensive republic, studded with cities, towns and prosperous farms and filled with all the blessings of liberty, civilization and religion?"

In 1846, William Gilpin—a writer, lawyer, and political leader—claimed that the "destiny of the American people is to subdue the continent—to rush over this vast field to the Pacific Ocean—to animate the many hundreds of millions of its people, to cheer them upward . . . to establish a new order in human affairs."

▲ Mission in Acoma Pueblo, New Mexico, in 1890. The Spanish forced Native Americans to follow Catholic traditions, such as celebrating feast days like this one. Some descendants of these Indian converts still practice Catholicism.

America by conquering the Incas and Aztecs who lived in the land that is now Peru and Mexico and by stealing their gold and jewels. Greedy for more wealth, Spain began establishing colonies there in 1519. At its peak, the Spanish empire ruled most of South and Central America, parts of the Caribbean, and present-day Mexico, Florida, and most of the Southwest territory.

The Spanish filled their labor needs by enslaving the conquered Native Americans. Additional slaves from Africa arrived on ships in coastal ports. At one time, more Africans lived in New Spain than Europeans. Many Africans and American Indians were cruelly forced to construct Spanish buildings, herd cattle, mine precious metals, and farm land. After years of Spanish colonization, the people of New Spain spoke mainly Spanish. Spanish-speaking people in California began calling themselves Californios.

Spanish Missions

Religion was important to the Spanish conquest of New Spain. Catholicism was the Spanish national religion, and Spaniards believed it was their duty to spread the Catholic belief system—by choice or by force. Missions were church complexes that served as the main Spanish frontier institutions. They existed to convert Native Americans and exploit their labor to work farm fields and ranches.

Missions in Mexico, South America, and Central America were built beginning in the 1500s. Mission building in what is now California began in the mid-1700s. Around that time, Spain needed safe California ports for its treasure-laden ships sailing to and from Asia.

Native Americans in the Missions

Some Native Americans entered missions voluntarily, but most were forced there and made to convert and work from dawn to dusk. Practicing Native ceremonies or religious or cultural traditions was forbidden, and those caught were severely punished. Some mission Indians adopted European religion, lan-

Pueblo Revolt

The Spanish called all Native Americans who lived in towns with multi-level homes in the Southwest the "Pueblo" people because the Spanish word for "town" is *pueblo*. In reality, the Pueblo consist of about twenty-five different groups, including the Hopi and Zuni.

The Pueblo and other Native groups were not happy with Spanish colonization. The Pueblo, tired of being forced to work in missions, often tried to fight the Spanish. In 1675, the Spanish arrested forty-seven of the Pueblo's religious leaders and charged them with sorcery and starting rebellions against Spain. Four leaders were hanged, and the rest were brutally whipped and then released.

One of the arrested leaders was Popé. After being released by the Spanish, he traveled from town to town planning a massive uprising of American Indians. In 1680, the Pueblo people executed a coordinated attack against several missions and settlements, driving the Spanish from New Mexico for more than a decade.

▲ Zuni pueblo in New Mexico in early 1900s. Pueblo architecture during the 1600s looked much like the elaborately tiered adobe buildings seen in this picture. Despite their advanced culture and well-developed towns, many of the Pueblo people were forced from their homes and put into Spanish missions to work.

guage, and customs, but others practiced their religion and culture in secret to keep it alive.

Many Native Americans died from diseases the Spaniards brought with them from Europe. The Indians had no natural resistance to foreign illnesses, such as smallpox and measles. In California, the Catholic Church claimed to have baptized about eighty-seven thousand Indians, but an estimated sixty-three thousand of the converts died.

Each mission was scheduled to become a pueblo (see p. 9) after ten years, free of church control. Native Americans would then become free Spanish citizens. Missions became so wealthy, however, that the Spanish never followed through with their plan.

Presidios

France, England, and Russia also had colonies in other areas of North America, and Spain protected its land claims by building

military forts called presidios. It was expensive to maintain remote presidios, so most housed only a few soldiers.

Each presidio had an open rectangular courtyard surrounded by buildings. These buildings included a small church, living quarters, storehouses, workshops, wells, and cisterns to store water. A high wall called a rampart circled and protected the entire presidio. Land around the presidio was set aside for farming and raising animals, but it was often hard to grow enough food for everyone in the fort.

Pueblos

To solve the food problem, Spain encouraged its people to form *pueblos,* or small towns, near presidios. The government offered new Spanish settlers a five-year break on taxes, free land, supplies, livestock, and a yearly allowance for buying clothes and other supplies. In exchange, settlers had to sell the extra food they produced to local presidios.

By 1800, New Spain was quite diverse. People of different ethnic or racial backgrounds had children together, effectively creating new ethnic groups, such as *mestizos* (people of Native American and European descent) and *mulattos* (people of African and European descent). The original eleven families recruited by the Spanish from New Spain to found Los Angeles included Spaniards, Blacks, mulattos, Indians, and mestizos.

▲ Mission churches, such as the ruins of this one built in 1797 at San Juan Capistrano mission in California (pictured in 1907), were often large and grand to convince Native Americans how powerful and rich the Catholic religion was. Today, historians are restoring the San Juan Capistrano mission, and the church is once again active.

Chapter 2

Mexico and the Southwest

By the early 1800s, after three hundred years of Spanish control, most Spanish colonists wanted freedom. Events in Spain made the colonists even more disconnected with their homeland. In 1808, French Emperor Napoleon Bonaparte invaded Spain, removed the Spanish king, and declared that his brother, Joseph Bonaparte, was the new king of Spain. Most colonists in New Spain felt they should not have to serve King Bonaparte.

Mexican Revolution (1810–1821)

In September 1810, Catholic priest Miguel Hidalgo started the Mexican Revolution by giving a fiery speech in his church in Dolores Hidalgo,

◀ Father Miguel Hidalgo led a volunteer army of about sixty thousand during the first battles of the Mexican Revolution. He was eventually killed by Spanish troops.

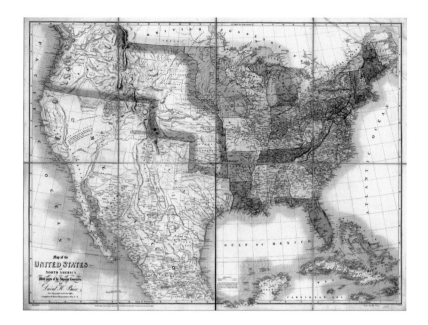

This historical map of North America shows the territory belonging to Mexico and the United States in 1839.

Mexico, that asked the residents of New Spain to rebel. He asked for volunteers to fight and led them into battles with Spanish troops. After years of bloody fighting, New Spain won its independence from Spain in 1821. The people named their new country Mexico.

Mexican territory included present-day Mexico as well as the land that is now Texas, California, New Mexico, Nevada, and Arizona. Officials in Mexico City appointed governors to manage Mexico's frontier provinces and to collect taxes. Management through appointed governors was not an easy task because people in the provinces wanted more control over their local governments.

The Mission System Ends

In 1834, Mexico passed a law that the missions finally be secularized, or taken out of church control. The Catholic Church kept only the religious buildings. Government administrators were in charge of dividing the remaining mission property. Half of it was to be divided among the Indians that lived there, and other Mexicans could buy the remaining land. Unfortunately, many American Indians did not receive property. Instead, the Mexican administrators sold the majority of the land and cattle to friends or wealthy families.

▶ Artist William Henry Jackson's c. 1880s rendering of a scene from a typical ranching hacienda in Mexico. Haciendas were like small towns in themselves—they included the ranchero's home, vaquero (cowhand) homes, stables, a mill, and sometimes a church and a blacksmith.

Native Americans who received land often did not keep it for long. Many were cheated by developers or sold the land to settlers. Without land or missions to work in, Native Americans were forced to take whatever low-paying jobs they could find.

The Rancho System Begins

The Mexican government sold or granted former mission land to individuals for forming ranchos, or ranches. Each grant was a maximum size of 50,000 acres (20,230 hectares) and came with a map showing its borders. Some landowners received multiple grants and created *haciendas,* huge estates that covered vast territories. They ruled their haciendas like kings.

Trading Hides for Goods

—Prudencia Higuera, the daughter of a ranchero, in a diary entry describing the trade between her family and a foreign trader.

" The next morning my father [the ranchero] gave orders, and my brothers, with the peons [menial laborers], went on horseback into the mountains and smaller valleys to round up all the best cattle. They drove them to the beach, killed them there, and salted the hides. They tried out the tallow in some iron kettles . . . . The captain soon came to our landing with a small boat and two sailors . . . . The captain looked over the hides, and then asked my father to get into the boat and go to the vessel . . . . [My father] came back the next day, bringing four boat-loads of cloth, axes, shoes, fish-lines, and many new things . . . . My brother had traded some deerskins for a gun and four tooth-brushes, the first ones I had ever seen. "

Sometimes rancheros and their families worked on ranchos, but usually the former mission Indians formed the rancho labor force. They were technically free, but they had few choices about how to make a living. They usually received no money for their work, only food, shelter, and clothing to survive.

Open Trade Policy

To help the country's economy, the Mexican government encouraged Mexicans to trade with foreigners, especially the Anglos from the United States. Anglos were white people of non-Spanish, European descent. Mexico's open trade policy brought increasing numbers of Anglo people from the United States to the Southwest. Fur traders came to hunt and trap in the area. Some traders arrived by ship to buy and sell goods. In 1841, the first settlers to come by wagon train overland arrived in California. A steady stream of Anglo immigrants followed. Mexico's northern provinces soon became home to a mix of Anglo, Spanish, Native American, and African peoples.

Californio Revolution of 1836

Relations between Mexico City and California reached a crisis in 1836. Unhappy with Mexican rule, Juan Bautista Alvarado—an inspector and local Monterey leader—led a group of Californios to revolt. They seized control of Monterey, the Mexican capital of California, and forced Mexican officials to leave. Alvarado then declared California a free and united country.

Mexico, however, did not want to lose such an important province and quickly appointed a new military governor. Alvarado and his supporters refused to recognize the new governor and defeated the Mexican forces seeking to install the new leader. To keep California and avoid further conflict, Mexican officials allowed Alvarado to assume the position of governor. In this powerful role, Alvarado managed California's affairs without deferring to Mexican authority. A new Mexican military representative finally managed to remove him from office in 1842.

The Jones Incident

In the 1840s, as more Anglos populated California, U.S.-Mexican relations became strained. The Anglos wanted Mexican land to become part of the United States. The U.S. military issued standing orders that troops were to immediately seize Monterey, the Mexican capital of California, if war broke out between the countries.

In 1842, a young officer named Commodore Thomas Jones heard that the United States and Mexico were at war. Without confirming the truth of the report, he followed the standing orders and took one hundred fifty marines and sailed for Monterey. The war party landed on Monterey beach on October 18 and demanded that the presidio surrender to the United States. It did, and Jones replaced the Mexican flag with the U.S. flag. He declared that California was now protected by the United States.

Jones had made a big mistake, however. The countries were not at war. As soon as he realized what he had done, Jones lowered the U.S. flag and left with the marines. He lost his command as a result of his rash action.

▲ Location of the presidio at Monterrey, shown here in 1938, where the Jones Incident occurred. When the U.S. government took over California, it built a new military fort to replace the old Spanish adobe presidio that once overlooked the bay at Monterey.

Chapter 3

The Southwest Becomes a U.S. Territory

The relationship between the United States and Mexico worsened in 1845 when Texas became a U.S. state. Texas had achieved independence from Mexico in 1836, but Mexico refused to officially acknowledge Texas's independence or its borders.

U.S. president James Polk sent John Slidell to Mexico in 1845 to buy California and New Mexico and to form an agreement finalizing Texas's border. Mexican officials refused even to talk to Slidell, and he left the country in 1846.

Mexican-American War

Polk sent troops to guard Texas's borders. Mexico believed this was an act of

◀ U.S. president James Polk made expansion an issue in his campaign and favored the annexation of Texas. Because of his beliefs, people questioned his motives for the Mexican-American War. Many thought it was just an excuse to grab more land.

Blood Shed on American Soil

—President Polk in a message to Congress asking to declare war on Mexico.

66 We have tried every effort at reconciliation. . . . But now, after reiterated menaces, Mexico has passed the boundary of the United States, has invaded our territory and shed American blood upon the American soil. She has proclaimed that hostilities have commenced, and that the two nations are at war. As war exists, and, notwithstanding all our efforts to avoid it, exists by the act of Mexico herself, we are called upon by every consideration of duty and patriotism to vindicate with decision the honor, the rights, and the interests of our country. 99

war. On April 24, 1846, the Mexican commander crossed the Rio Grande River and battled a group of American scouts, killing or wounding sixteen of them.

In response, on May 13, the United States declared war on Mexico. U.S. troops invaded Mexico, crossing the Rio Grande and capturing three of Mexico's provincial capital cities. U.S. General Stephen Watts Kearny and his men marched to Santa Fe, where they defeated a force of four thousand Mexicans and Indians to assume control of what is now the state of New Mexico.

California and the War

About two thousand American settlers lived in California when the Mexican-American War started. On June 14, 1846, a band of about thirty American settlers rebelled and captured Mexican leaders in Sonoma, California. William Todd, the nephew of future president Abraham Lincoln, made a flag for the rebels, with a bear, a star, and the words "California Republic." The rebels flew the flag and declared California an independent republic. The incident became known as the Bear Flag Revolt.

▲ John Frémont pictured at some point between 1855 and 1865.

U.S. Army Lieutenant Colonel John Frémont, who was leading an army exploring expedition in northern California, traveled south to Sonoma with his troops and assumed leadership of the Bear Flag Revolt. He named the joint forces the California Battalion and assumed temporary governorship of California.

The California Republic did not last long. On July 9, 1846, U.S. naval forces arrived and claimed California as part of the United States. Several large battles occurred after Mexican leaders in California asked Californios to show the world "an example of loyalty and firmness" by fighting the U.S. invaders.

Most Californios, however, did not offer much resistance to the U.S. occupation, and fighting in California ended before the war was officially over. Mexican forces in California surrendered to Frémont on January 13, 1847.

Treaty of Guadalupe Hidalgo

The war formally ended on February 2, 1848, when officials from both countries signed the Treaty of Guadalupe Hidalgo. In it, the United States agreed to give Mexico $15 million and to pay about $3.2 million worth of Mexico's debts. In return, Mexico agreed to recognize the Rio Grande as Texas's border and to give the United States about half of Mexico's territory.

▼ This map shows the borders of Mexico and the United States before and after the Mexican-American War.

The Mexican-American War

UNITED STATES

N

- Sonoma
- Monterey
- Los Angeles X
  Jan 9, 1847
- X San Pasqual
  Dec. 6, 1846
- San Diego
- X Santa Fe
  Aug. 18, 1846
- X El Brazito
  Dec. 25, 1846

MEXICO

Pacific Ocean

Rio Grande

Nueces

Monterrey X
Sept. 21-24, 1846

X Palo Alto
May 8, 1846
Matamoros

X
Buena Vista
Feb. 23, 1847

Mexico City
Sept. 14, 1847
X

Vera Cruz
Mar. 29, 1847
X

LEGEND

~~	River
●	Major City
X	Major Battle
-------	1848 Boundary
-------	1819 Boundary

0   200 mi
0   300 km

▶ This cartoon illustrates the heated debate about slavery. Proslavery politicians are forcing a slave down the throat of an abolitionist, also known as a free-soiler.

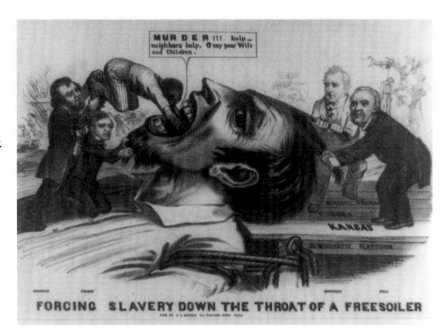

FORCING SLAVERY DOWN THE THROAT OF A FREESOILER

▼ African American workers picking cotton about 1900. After slavery was outlawed, free African Americans had difficulty finding jobs. Many could only find work doing what they had done as slaves, tending cotton.

Issues Facing the New U.S. Territory

It took the U.S. government some time to decide how to govern its new lands. Before an area could become a territory or state, it had to have a certain population. Then, residents had to draft a constitution and submit it to Congress. Congress then voted on whether to accept or reject an area as a territory or state. This process could be difficult and lengthy, and some territories tried unsuccessfully for many years to become states.

Also, in the mid-1800s, the issue of slavery divided the country. Thousands of slaves were forced to work in the plantations and mines of the South. Southern states believed that slavery should continue to be allowed, while many Northern states outlawed it and felt it should be outlawed throughout the nation. While congressional leaders argued whether slavery should be allowed in the Southwest, the new territory was temporarily without formal government.

The Grand Canyon is the most famous geographical landmark of the Southwest. John Wesley Powell, a geologist and one-armed Civil War hero, was the first to travel the length of the Grand Canyon on the dangerous Colorado River. In May 1869, Powell set off with nine men, supplies, and boats. The rough rapids quickly claimed several boats and most of their supplies. One month into the trip, one of his companions quit, saying "I have had more excitement than a man deserves in a lifetime." One month after this, three men decided to climb out of the Grand Canyon instead of continuing on the river. They told Powell, "We surely will all die if we continue on this journey."

Still, Powell refused to quit exploring the canyon. He and his five remaining companions completed their exploration of the river on August 29. They had been gone for three months and were assumed to be dead. After his triumphant return, Powell toured the country giving talks about his discoveries.

Powell's expedition formed the groundwork for future exploration of the Grand Canyon. He later became the head of the U.S. Geographical Survey in 1881, an organization that maps the terrain of the United States.

Chapter 4

The Gold Rush and California Statehood

California had been a U.S. territory only for one year when an accidental discovery forever changed its population, history, and culture.

Gold Discovered

On January 24, 1848, a carpenter named James Marshall saw gold shining in the streaming water of Sutter's Mill on the American River. Merchant Sam Brannan had a shop near the mill and used Marshall's discovery to draw customers. He walked San Francisco's streets, yelling, "Gold! Gold! Gold from the American River." When people gathered, Brannan showed them

◀ This hand-tinted 1890 photo shows a miner panning for gold in northern California.

THE WAY THEY GO TO CALIFORNIA.

◀ This 1849 cartoon makes fun of the forty-niners and their frantic race to get to the California gold fields in the fastest transportation they could find.

gold nuggets as proof. San Franciscans then raced to the American River to find their own gold, and many of them stopped at Brannan's store to buy supplies. The Gold Rush had begun, and California was never the same.

About ninety thousand more miners—known as "forty-niners"—flooded the area in 1849. About 80 percent were Anglo Americans from other areas of the United States. The rest of the miners traveled from Europe, Australia, China, Hawaii, Mexico, Peru, and Chile. The new arrivals quickly made California one of the most ethnically diverse places on Earth.

Rise of Boomtowns

When greedy gold seekers arrived, some stole Native American land and forced the Indians to mine for them. Other newcomers settled on rancho land as "squatters." Wherever gold was found, a mining camp, or boomtown, sprouted on the spot.

San Francisco was one of the first and largest boomtowns. A newcomer named Bayard Taylor described what he saw in 1849

San Francisco; "Hundreds of tents and houses . . . On every side stood buildings of all kinds, begun or half-finished, and the greater part of them mere canvas sheds, open in front and covered with all kinds of signs in all languages. Great quantities of goods were piled in the open air, for want of a place to store them. The streets were full of people, hurrying to and fro, and of divers [sic] and bizarre a character as the houses. One knows not whether he is awake or in some wonderful dream."

▼ This 1890s photo shows the typical shops and streets of a boomtown in the West.

Miners abandoned most boomtowns as soon as the gold was gone, but some of the larger towns, such as Sacramento and San Francisco, are still thriving today.

Decline of Ranchos

In 1848, ranchos still covered about 13 million acres (5 million ha) of California because the Treaty of Guadalupe Hidalgo guaranteed the property rights of Mexican rancheros. Many gold seekers, however, ignored these rights and moved onto rancho land. Hungry miners stole cattle and animals to eat. As the rancheros were losing their land and their livelihood, they turned to the U.S. government for help.

In 1851, Congress passed a new land law that gave rancheros the right to forcibly remove the squatters and prove the validity of their rancho land titles in court. This legal procedure, however, was costly and took as long as seventeen years. By the time the cases were settled, most rancheros were already bankrupt and could no longer afford to keep their land.

Gold Rush Law and Discrimination

Since government institutions were not yet in place, many boomtowns had no organized law. Miners banded together to punish whomever they suspected of committing crimes. Frontier justice was harsh and victims often were beaten or put to death with no trials.

Miners formed more than five hundred democratic mining districts to protect their gold and land claims. One person was elected to record claims and settle disputes. The district miners also wrote a code, or set of rules, governing matters such as the size of a claim.

Anglo miners voted on how to manage the district, but minority groups had no control. Districts also often discriminated against African Americans, Native Americans, and foreign miners, such as the Chinese and French. These miners had to pay special taxes to be allowed to mine. Several times

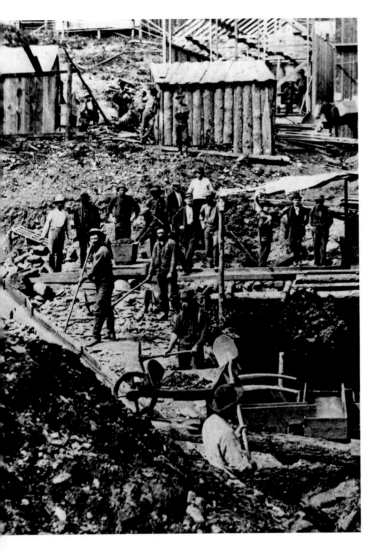

▲ California prospectors were the first to take Native American land for gold mining, but they were not the last. These miners in South Dakota are mining for gold in the Black Hills, sacred Sioux land.

mobs of Anglo miners killed Chinese miners or forced them to leave town. Many Native American claims were unfairly taken away and given to Anglo miners.

Native American rights were especially abused during the Gold Rush. Since much of the gold was on Native American land, some gold seekers killed Native Americans to get it. This quote, offensive and racist by today's standards, from the *Chico Courant* newspaper describes how some people felt: "It is a mercy to the red devils to exterminate them, and a saving of many white lives." About one hundred fifty thousand Native Americans lived in California in 1848. By 1870, there were only about thirty thousand Native Americans left.

Statehood

With the boom in population, California residents soon wanted a legal government. The Gold Rush had made California's population so large that they asked to be admitted immediately as a state, skipping territorial status, which usually came first. In 1849, they wrote a constitution, voted to outlaw slavery, and were the first to grant property rights to married women.

California's request to become a free state, however, sparked one of Congress's greatest debates. Southern senators were upset because, with California's addition, there would be one more free state than slave state. After much arguing, Congress finally agreed to the Compromise of 1850. It approved California's entry into the union as a free state, but it also passed a strict fugitive slave law, making it easier for owners to capture runaway slaves.

On September 9, 1850, President Millard Fillmore signed a bill admitting California into the Union as a state. It took five weeks for the news to reach California. The SS *Oregon* sailed into San Francisco Bay on October 18 with all its flags flying to signal California had achieved statehood.

Biddy Mason (1818–1891)

Biddy Mason was an African American hero who influenced the early development of California. She was born into slavery on a Mississippi plantation owned by Robert Smith on August 15, 1818. She eventually had three daughters—Ellen, Ann, and Harriet.

In 1851, Smith moved his household, including slaves, to California. Slavery was illegal there, and so Mason took Smith to court, demanding freedom for herself and her daughters. Mason won her case in 1856 and was set free.

Eager to start her new life, Mason moved to Los Angeles and worked long hours as a nurse. She saved her money and became the first African American woman to buy land in Los Angeles. She developed the land and grew rich from her real-estate holdings.

Mason helped her community by visiting jails and giving money to many different charities. Lines of people formed outside her house because she was known for feeding, clothing, and housing hundreds of needy people. Mason was also one of the founders of the First African Methodist Episcopal Church, the first African American church in Los Angeles. She died on January 15, 1891.

Chapter 5

Nevada Statehood

The landscape of what is now Nevada is shaped by the 189,000-square mile (489,500-sq km) Great Basin, which covers all but the eastern and southern edges of the state. Few rivers cut through this elevated region of mountains, valleys, and deserts.

Native American groups lived in the Great Basin for thousands of years, but its landscape and climate was a challenge to European settlement. Other than a few Spanish explorers, Europeans stayed out of the area until the 1820s, when fur traders began arriving in the region.

Utah Territory

In 1850, Congress created the Utah Territory, which included present-day Utah and all but the southern tip of what is now Nevada. Most of the territory's first settlers were members of the

◀ This 1855 lithograph of Great Basin Valley shows what the landscape there looked like in the mid-1800s.

The Mormon pioneers coming off Big Mountain into Mountain Dell. July 1847.

Church of Jesus Christ of Latter-Day Saints, also called Mormons. Many people in the United States disagreed with Mormon teachings and abused its followers. To escape the abuse, Mormon leader Brigham Young organized one of the largest migrations in history. He guided his Mormon followers to the Great Salt Lake area, where they settled and founded Salt Lake City. When the area became a territory, Salt Lake City was named its capital, and Young served as its first governor until 1857.

▲ Brigham Young (inset photo) led a mass migration of Mormon wagon trains (top) out West. When he saw the Great Salt Lake area, he stopped and said, "This is the right place."

Traveling through Nevada

One of the main routes to the West was the California Trail, which followed the Humboldt River as it passed through what is now Nevada. After gold was discovered in California in 1848, about twenty-five thousand people journeyed through Nevada.

For most people, the trip started in late spring in Independence, Missouri. One-fourth of the trip was spent crossing

In 1860, a transportation pioneer named William Russell created a relay system of mail delivery called the Pony Express. Its purpose was to quickly bring mail from Missouri through the Rocky Mountains to California. A letter took about ten and one-half days to travel from St. Joseph to Sacramento.

To do this, Russell built stations 5 to 15 miles (8 to 24 km) apart. At swing stations, Pony Express riders switched their tired horses for fresh ones. At home stations, riders rested, ate, and slept. A large part of the mail route passed through present-day Nevada, so Russell built many stations there.

The job was dangerous, as this advertisement suggests: "Wanted: Young, skinny, wiry fellows not over eighteen. Must be expert riders, willing to risk death daily. Orphans preferred." Riders traveled about 75 miles (121 km) each day and earned $100 a month.

The legendary Pony Express operated only for one and one-half years. On October 24, 1861, construction finished on the transcontinental telegraph line. The telegraph sent messages so quickly that there was no longer a need for the Pony Express.

Nevada. Along the Humboldt River, travelers dealt with poor water, dust clouds, lack of food, and steep canyons. Settlers could not stop long because they had less than one hundred thirty days to travel about 2,000 miles (3,219 km). If they were not in California by October, they risked being trapped in the snowy mountain passes of the Sierra Nevada Mountains.

The California Trail through Nevada was the most-traveled trail. An estimated two hundred thousand people crossed it between 1840 and 1860. It was so popular that the mail was also transported along this route by stagecoach, and Congress made the trail a Federal Wagon Road in 1857.

The Comstock Lode

By 1859, prospectors began looking for gold in Carson Valley, Nevada. An adventurer named Henry Comstock noticed the miners were striking gold and falsely claimed that they were digging on his land. Rather than argue, the miners agreed to become partners with him. They began finding several hundred dollars worth of gold each day but complained about the heavy blue "sand" they had to dig through to remove the gold-filled rock.

One prospector took a sack of the blue material to be analyzed and discovered it was remarkably pure silver. The mineral-rich lode was named Comstock Lode after Henry Comstock, and it proved to be one of the richest mineral discoveries in U.S. history.

News of the silver strike quickly spread. Thousands of prospectors swarmed into Nevada from California, bringing

◀ This miner is using a hammer and spike to chisel rock from the Comstock Mine in Virginia City, Nevada, in 1867. Miners would eventually extract about $400 million in silver from the Comstock Lode.

▲ Boomtowns in Nevada, such as Gold Hill, pictured above in 1867, at first consisted of shanties, tents, wagons, and temporary houses made of branches. Some men even lived in coyote holes.

California's mining business to a standstill. Nevada boomtowns, such as Silver City, Gold Hill, and Virginia City, quickly formed. Virginia City became the second-largest city in the West, boasting a population of almost thirty thousand and the first elevator—called a "rising room"—in the frontier.

Investors bought land from the original prospectors and opened mines in different locations along the lode. Mine after mine struck it rich. In a short time, land value rose from $1 to $4,000 per foot.

The Nevada Territory and Statehood

People who settled in present-day Nevada, in the western region of the Utah Territory, were miners or businesspeople, not

Mormons. They wanted to sepa-
rate and form a new territory.
Without Congress's approval,
local leaders met in 1859 and
declared that they had left the
Utah Territory and were now the
Nevada Territory. After many
debates in Congress, the Nevada
Territory was created in March
1861.

President Abraham Lincoln
used the Nevada Territory to help
the Union war effort during the
Civil War. He encouraged the
territorial government to apply
for statehood, even though
Nevada did not have the required
population. Lincoln was in such
a hurry that the entire proposed
constitution was sent to Congress
by telegraph.

President Lincoln officially
made Nevada the thirty-sixth
state on October 31, 1864. He
used $45 million worth of silver
from Nevada's mines to help sup-
ply the Union army.

▶ President Lincoln, shown here inspecting Union
troops during the Civil War, needed Nevada's vote
to help him pass the Thirteenth Amendment that
outlawed slavery.

Chapter 6

Oklahoma Statehood

I n 1803, the United States bought 825,000 square miles (2,137,000 sq km) of land, including what is now Oklahoma, from France in the Louisiana Purchase. To govern the area, the U.S. government broke the purchase into territories. Oklahoma was made part of the Arkansas Territory in 1819.

In the 1800s, Anglo Americans wanted to settle on Native American land, and the Indians fought to protect their territory. To protect Anglo settlement, the U.S. government adopted a harsh policy of Indian removal and resettlement, forcing Native Americans to leave their homelands and settle out West.

The Indian Removal Act of 1830 gave the U.S. president power to choose land to set aside for Native Americans. President Andrew Jackson

◀ A U.S. soldier guards Native prisoners who were arrested and forced onto a reservation for fighting U.S. troops in the mid-1800s. Many Native Americans resisted removal from their homelands.

designated a large part of the Louisiana Purchase, including Oklahoma, for Native American resettlement in 1835. The U.S. Army gathered thousands of Native Americans and cruelly forced them onto reservations in Indian Territory in present-day Oklahoma. The Cherokee Nation removal was especially harsh. During 1838 to 1839, the U.S. Army made about fifteen thousand Cherokee travel by boat or walk the 1,000-mile (1,609-km) trip to Indian Territory. Suffering from lack of food or shelter, about four thousand Cherokee died on the freezing "Nunahi-duna-dlo-hilu-I." Translated, this means the "Trail Where They Cried" or the "Trail of Tears."

The American Indian survivors mourned the loss of their traditional homelands in the southeast but managed to form new settlements among the other Native American groups already living in the Indian Territory, beginning what many call the Indian Territory's "Golden Age."

Cruel and Unjust

—From a petition from Cherokee women to their tribal leadership to protest selling their land and moving to Indian Territory, October 17, 1821.

❝ We believe the present plan of the General Government to effect our removal West of the Mississippi, and thus obtain our lands for the use of the State of Georgia, to be highly oppressive, cruel and unjust. And we sincerely hope there is no consideration which can induce our citizens to forsake the land of our fathers of which they have been in possession from time immemorial, and thus compel us, against our will, to undergo the toils and difficulties of removing with our helpless families hundreds of miles to unhealthy and unproductive country. We hope therefore the Committee and Council will take into deep consideration our deplorable situation, and do everything in their power to avert such a state of things. And we trust by a prudent course their transactions with the General Government will enlist in our behalf the sympathies of the good people of the United States. ❞

Boomers

The Homestead Act of 1862 jeopardized Indian Territory by making settlement out West even more attractive to Anglos. The act granted 160 acres (65 ha) of public land to legal settlers for free if they farmed and improved it for five years.

As the U.S. population grew, some people, called boomers, wanted to open Indian Territory to non-Indian settlement. In 1879, boomers began illegally settling in the region. They were all evicted, fined $1,000, or arrested by U.S. troops.

In 1887, Congress passed the Dawes Act, which eliminated traditional Native American homelands. It forced Native Americans to break up their lands and accept just 160 acres (65 ha) per individual tribe member. This new way of dividing land left about 2 million acres (809,400 ha) of the Indian Territory without Native American owners. These acres became known as Unassigned Lands. Boomers wanted to settle this area, too.

Native Americans tried to protect their land by fighting the boomers in court. This legal opposition worked temporarily, but eventually the government gave in to public demand. In 1889, President Benjamin Harrison approved opening the Unassigned Lands for settlement.

▼ A boomer family being escorted from the Unassigned Lands by U.S. troops. Illustration is from an 1885 edition of *Harper's Weekly*, a popular weekly news periodical of the era.

◀ An 1893 photo of the Oklahoma land rush. Settlers are lined up and waiting for the official signal opening the land to settlement. Some settlers rode horses or trains into unclaimed territory, while others drove covered wagons.

First train leaving the line north of Orlembo for Perry Sept 16 1893

Oklahoma Territory

At noon on April 22, 1889, military officers signaled the opening of the Unassigned Lands for settlement. Immediately, about fifty thousand people on wagons, trains, or horses dashed into the territory in a wild race to claim one of the twelve thousand available homesteads. People who sneaked into the territory and claimed homesteads before the official opening were nicknamed "sooners."

Settlers in the Unassigned Lands had no formal government for one year. In 1890, Congress officially made the lands the Oklahoma Territory, and a territorial government was appointed. Together, the Oklahoma and Indian Territories became known as the Twin Territories.

The land grab, however, was not over. The U.S. government continued buying or taking away land from Native American nations. The land rushes of 1891, 1893, 1901, and 1911 redistrib-

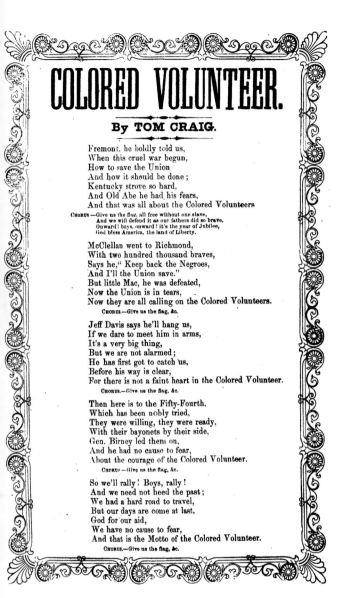

COLORED VOLUNTEER.

By TOM CRAIG.

Fremont, he boldly told us,
When this cruel war begun,
How to save the Union
And how it should be done ;
Kentucky strove so hard,
And Old Abe he had his fears,
And that was all about the Colored Volunteers

CHORUS.—Give us the flag, all free without one slave,
And we will defend it as our fathers did so brave,
Onward! boys, onward ! it's the year of Jubilee,
God bless America, the land of Liberty.

McClellan went to Richmond,
With two hundred thousand braves,
Says he," Keep back the Negroes,
And I'll the Union save."
But little Mac, he was defeated,
Now the Union is in tears,
Now they are all calling on the Colored Volunteers.

CHORUS.—Give us the flag, &c.

Jeff Davis says he'll hang us,
If we dare to meet him in arms,
It's a very big thing,
But we are not alarmed ;
He has first got to catch us,
Before his way is clear,
For there is not a faint heart in the Colored Volunteer.

CHORUS.—Give us the flag, &c.

Then here is to the Fifty-Fourth,
Which has been nobly tried,
They were willing, they were ready,
With their bayonets by their side,
Gen. Birney led them on,
And he had no cause to fear,
About the courage of the Colored Volunteer.

CHORUS.—Give us the flag, &c.

So we'll rally ! Boys, rally !
And we need not heed the past ;
We had a hard road to travel,
But our days are come at last,
God for our aid,
We have no cause to fear,
And that is the Motto of the Colored Volunteer.

CHORUS.—Give us the flag, &c.

▲ This broadside ballad from the 1860s praises a regiment of Buffalo Soldiers for their accomplishments during the Civil War.

uted even more former Indian land to homesteaders.

African Americans

The first African American settlers in Oklahoma were slaves of the Native American groups in the Indian Territory. They were freed after the Civil War, and the Dawes Act later granted them tribal land. Many African Americans also claimed free land under the Homestead Act during the land-rush years.

African Americans also founded about twenty-seven all-Black towns in the territory. Some nearby Anglo settlers refused to hire, trade, or sell anything to African Americans. Despite discrimination, some African American towns continued to prosper.

During the Civil War, many African Americans joined the Union army to fight for freedom. The army formed six all-Black regiments, which were later consolidated to two. After the war, these regiments were assigned to serve in the West, including Oklahoma, where they were nicknamed "Buffalo Soldiers" by the Native Americans they fought. While stationed at forts in Indian Territory from

1866 to 1898, Buffalo Soldiers protected Native Americans from boomers, helped build telegraph lines, protected railroad workers and settlers, patrolled reservations, and fought during Native American uprisings.

▲ An 1890 photo of African American soldiers (also known as "Buffalo Soldiers") from the Twenty-fifth Infantry Division.

Statehood

The Twin Territories' population increased when a huge oil field called Glenn Pool was discovered in 1905. It was one of the richest oil fields ever known, producing millions of barrels of crude oil. Tulsa—a boomtown that became known as the oil capital of the world—was soon full of people hoping to profit from the oil strike.

The land rushes and oil strike had brought so many people to the Twin Territories that they met the population requirement for statehood. In 1905, Indian and Anglo leaders from both territories worked together to draft a constitution. The territories joined together and officially became the state of Oklahoma on November 16, 1907.

Chapter 7

Arizona and New Mexico Become States

What is now Arizona and New Mexico became the property of Mexico after it won independence from Spain in 1821. The most important change under the Mexican government was the open trade policy that encouraged use of the Santa Fe Trail, a transportation route stretching from Independence, Missouri, through Arizona, to Santa Fe, New Mexico. Each year, increasing numbers of merchandise caravans made the about 800-mile (1,290-km) trip to Santa Fe, and in 1850, a monthly stagecoach line began traveling the trail. Towns also formed along the trail.

◀ The remains of the adobe Fort Union in New Mexico, a popular stop along the Santa Fe Trail. U.S. Army troops stationed at the fort helped defend the Santa Fe Trail.

U.S. Territory

Most of present-day Arizona and New Mexico became U.S. property after the Mexican-American War. People in the territory quickly began working to become a state. The territory's government drafted an antislavery constitution, but Congress denied the area statehood because Southerners in Congress did not want to admit another free state. Instead, the government created the New Mexico Territory in 1850, which included most of present-day New Mexico and Arizona.

President Franklin Pierce added more land to the New Mexico Territory in the 1853 Gadsden Purchase. For $10 million, U.S. agent James Gadsden bought from Mexico a 30,000 square mile (77,700 sq km) strip of land stretching through southern New Mexico and Arizona. Ten years later, President Lincoln split the New Mexico Territory nearly in half and created the Arizona Territory.

▼ To help maintain order, the U.S. government built military forts in its new territories. Below, Apache workers are bringing hay to soldiers stationed in Arizona Territory at the U.S. Fort Apache in 1893.

Apache Indians
Delivering Hay
93

The "Wild West"

The two territories' huge area proved hard to govern, and people soon considered the region wild and lawless. Bands of outlaws frequently robbed trains, banks, and stagecoaches. Gunfights, hangings, and murders were common.

Wars with Native Americans in Arizona and New Mexico also fueled this belief in the "Wild West." The U.S. Army built forts throughout the territory and forcibly moved them onto reservations. Sometimes the Indians, especially the Apache and Navajo, tried to defend their land by fighting. The last major conflict ended in 1886, when the great Apache Chief Geronimo surrendered to U.S. forces and entered a reservation.

Violent disagreements between ranchers and settlers also contributed to the general lawlessness. Cattle barons owned huge ranches that covered the grasslands. Squatters illegally settled on these lands, putting up fences and plowing the open range to create farms. Rustlers stole large numbers of cattle. In response, ranchers hired armed guards and cowhands to protect their cattle and their interests, which resulted in frequent gunfights with rustlers, squatters, authorities, and the gangs of rival cattle barons.

▲ This 1896 picture of a cattle ranch in Grant County, Arizona, shows a cowhand with a lassoed steer.

Statehood

Both Arizona and New Mexico wanted to change their "Wild-West" reputations and repeatedly tried to earn statehood. Finally, in 1910, President William Howard Taft signed an act allowing the New Mexico and Arizona Territories to hold constitutional conventions. Delegates from each territory met and wrote constitutions.

New Mexico voters approved a new state constitution in January 1911. One year later, on January 6, 1912, President Taft signed a law admitting New Mexico as the forty-seventh state. He told the New Mexican representatives, "Well, it is all over. I am glad to give you life. I hope you will be healthy."

Arizona voters approved their state constitution on February 9, 1911. The constitution allowed for the recall of judges who were not doing a good job. President Taft was against the recall of judges and refused to grant statehood until they took this provision out of the constitution. Arizona changed its constitution, and President Taft signed the proclamation making Arizona a state on February 14, 1912. After becoming the forty-eighth state, Arizona showed its independence by amending its constitution to once again allow the recall of judges.

Hawaii— A Legacy of Manifest Destiny

Manifest Destiny created a feeling of nationalism in the developing United States. Americans rallied to spread the U.S. form of government and conquer new territory. In the process, different regions of the country became interdependent on each other for goods. People began to think of themselves as Americans—working together to conquer a frontier.

After the United States established settlements throughout the West, Americans were left without a frontier to conquer. They soon became interested in islands in the Pacific. Since the early 1800s, American businesspeople had been acquiring Hawaii's sugarcane and sandalwood to trade. American missionaries began arriving in the 1820s to build schools and churches. As commercial ties increased, the United States began exerting more influence over the island government, even obtaining permission to build the Pearl Harbor Naval Base there. In 1893, American merchants helped overthrow Hawaii's ruler, Queen Liliuokalani. Hawaii was annexed in 1898 and made a territory in 1900. It became a state on August 21, 1959.

Thousands of Americans believing in Manifest Destiny risked their lives to move to the West, making the United States one of the largest countries in the world. They traveled far and wide to build railroads, telegraph lines, roads, cities, and establish their own form of government.

Despite these accomplishments, western expansion came at a high price. The U.S. government broke treaties and sacrificed many lives in wars fought to acquire territory. Settlers stole land and participated in the mass killing of American Indians. American progress, then, came at the tragic expense of Native American lives and prosperity.

Today, the West is a highly developed, populous region of the United States, but many Westerners still celebrate the frontier roots of their states. Much of the imagery of the "Wild West" has been romanticized in countless songs, books, and movies. Western history has been preserved in national parks and trails, and tourists journey to these places to experience the rich past of the American frontier. For better or worse, Manifest Destiny shaped the United States into the country it is today.

▼ These posters are advertising plays, movies, and shows that celebrate the "Wild West."

1492: ▶ Columbus lands in the Americas and claims the land for Spain.

1598: ▶ Juan de Oñate establishes first settlement in what is now New Mexico.

1680: ▶ Pueblo Indians revolt and expel the Spanish from area of New Mexico.

1769: ▶ First California mission is founded.

1803: ▶ The United States doubles its size with land bought in the Louisiana Purchase.

1810: ▶ Mexican Revolution begins after Miguel Hidalgo gives a speech calling for rebellion from Spain.

1821: ▶ Mexico wins independence from Spain, and the Mexican Revolution ends.

1823: ▶ President Monroe declares American intentions of expansion in a speech known as the Monroe Doctrine.

1830: ▶ Congress passes the Indian Removal Act, which legalized the removal and resettlement of Native American groups.

1836: ▶ Californios revolt against Mexican authority and appoint their own governor.

1838-1839: ▶ Thousands of Cherokees and other Native people die on the Trail of Tears.

1845: ▶ John O'Sullivan first uses term Manifest Destiny; Texas becomes a state.

1846: ▶ Mexican-American War begins; Americans declare that California is a free country after the Bear Flag Revolt.

1848: ▶ January 24—James Marshall finds gold at Sutter's Mill. February 2—Mexican-American War ends when Treaty of Guadalupe Hidalgo is signed.

1850: ▶ California becomes a state.

1853: ▶ The United States buys more land from Mexico in the Gadsden Purchase.

1859: ▶ Comstock Lode is discovered in Nevada.

1860: ▶ The Pony Express begins delivering mail.

1862: ▶ The Homestead Act—granting free land to settlers who farm and improve it for five years—becomes law.

1864: ▶ Nevada becomes a state.

1869: ▶ John Wesley Powell explores the Grand Canyon via the Colorado River.

1886: ▶ Apache Chief Geronimo surrenders to U.S. forces in New Mexico.

1887: ▶ Native American traditional homelands are eliminated when Congress passes the Dawes Act.

1889: ▶ The Unassigned Lands in Indian Territory open for non-Indian settlement.

1890: ▶ Congress forms the Oklahoma Territory.

1898: ▶ United States annexes Hawaii.

1907: ▶ Oklahoma becomes a state.

1912: ▶ New Mexico and Arizona become states.

1959: ▶ Hawaii becomes a state.

adobe: building material made of mud mixed with straw and then dried in the sun

Anglo: person of non-Spanish, European descent

colony: area, settlement, or country owned or controlled by another nation

discrimination: unfair treatment of an individual or group because of race, gender, or economic status

empire: political power that controls large territory, usually consisting of colonies or other nations

frontier: edge of known or settled land

hacienda: a huge estate formed by a Spanish government land grant, usually used for mining, ranching, or farming

lode: deposit of mineral in rock that contains valuable material, such as gold or silver

manifest: obviously true and easily recognizable. The term Manifest Destiny meant that the true and obvious destiny of the United States was to expand its borders to the Pacific Ocean.

mestizo: person of Native American and Spanish descent

mission: center built to establish Spanish settlement, convert Native Americans to Catholicism, and exploit their slave labor

mulatto: people of African and European descent

presidio: military fort built by the Spanish

prospector: person who explores an area looking for mineral resources

province: district of a nation that usually has its own capital town and some form of local government, similar to states of the United States

pueblo: Spanish word for town; the term also refers collectively to the tribes of Native Americans from Arizona and New Mexico that form the Pueblo people

republic: nation that has no sovereign or other unelected ruler but is led by a leader, or group of officials led by its citizens

secularize: make non-religious

territory: a subdivision of the United States that is not a state and is administered by an appointed or elected governor and elected legislature

trapper: hunter who uses traps to kill animals, such as beaver or squirrel, for their fur

treaty: agreement made between two or more people or groups of people after negotiation, usually at the end of a period of conflict

Books

Anderson, Dale. *The California Missions*. Landmark Events in American History (series). Milwaukee: World Almanac Library, 2002.

Barnett, Tracy. *Buffalo Soldiers*. Philadelphia: Mason Crest, 2002.

Faber, Harold. *John Charles Frémont: Pathfinder to the West*. Great Expectations (series). New York: Benchmark Books, 2003.

Johnson, Michael, and Bill Yenne. *Native Tribes of California and the Southwest*. Native Tribes of North America (series). Milwaukee: World Almanac Library, 2004.

Jones, Charlotte Foltz. *Westward Ho!: Eleven Explorers of the American West*. New York: Holiday House, 2004.

Uschan, Michael. *Westward Expansion*. World History (series). San Diego: Lucent Books, 2001.

World Almanac Library of the States (series). Milwaukee: World Almanac Library, 2002.

Web Sites

Buffalo Soldiers National Museum
www.buffalosoldiermuseum.com

California Gold Rush at Oakland Museum
www.museumca.org/goldrush.html

California Historical Society
www.californiahistoricalsociety.org

Kingwood College: American Cultural History
kclibrary.nhmccd.edu/ 19thcentury1880.htm

Museum of the Cherokee Indian
cherokeemuseum.org

Museum of Westward Expansion
*www.nps.gov/jeff/ expansion_museum.htm*man